This covered bridge crosses a small river

Bridges

Joanne Mattern

A⁺
Smart Apple Media

❖ Published by Smart Apple Media

1980 Lookout Drive, North Mankato, MN 56003

Designed by Rita Marshall

Printed in the United States of America

❖ Photographs by Richard Cummins, Dennis Frates, Galyn C. Hammond, The Image Finders (William Manning, Jim Yokatjy), Bruce Leighty, Gunter Marx Photography, Witold Skrypczak

❖ Library of Congress Cataloging-in-Publication Data

Mattern, Joanne, 1963- Bridges / by Joanne Mattern. p. cm. – (Structures)

Includes bibliographical references and index.

Summary: Discusses the purpose, design, and construction of bridges.

❖ ISBN 1-58340-150-4

1. Bridges–Juvenile literature. [1. Bridges.]. I. Title. II. Structures (North Mankato, Minn.)

TG148 .M38 2002   624.2–dc21   2001049972

❖ First Edition 9 8 7 6 5 4 3 2 1

Bridges

The History of Bridges

Bridges carry people, animals, cars, trains, and much more across water and deep valleys. They help people move goods easily from place to place. But that was not always the case. Before there were well-built bridges, people used steppingstones or rafts to cross streams or rivers. They often crossed canyons on fallen trees. ❖ One of the first bridges was built across the Euphrates River in Southwest Asia in 2200 B.C. The simple design used wooden planks placed on piles of rocks called piers (PEERZ). The piers formed islands in the

water. River water was **diverted** while the piers were being

built. When the bridge was completed, the water was allowed

to return to its normal path.

Many old bridges were built on rocky piers

Cables and Arches

Today, there are many different kinds of bridges, including beam, **arch**, and suspension. The beam bridge is a flat surface that rests on supports at each end. Think of a beam bridge as a piece of wood resting on two stones. ❖ In about 100 A.D., bridge builders began to build arch bridges. These bridges look like upside-down U's. Early arch bridges were made by stacking stones around a wooden frame to form a curved shape. Later, the Romans built flat decks on top of several arches to create longer bridges. ❖ By the end of the

1700s, builders were using cast iron to make arches. The iron

was much stronger than wood or stone. A century later, steel

wire was invented. John Roebling, a famous **engineer**, found a

An ancient Roman bridge built with several arches

Arches can be built over roads instead of under them

way to make thick metal ropes called cables out of these wires.

His cable was eventually used to build suspension bridges.

❖ Suspension bridges are made by hanging, or suspending, the roadway from cables. The cables are attached to bridge towers. From a distance, these bridges, with their drooping cables, look like jump ropes suspended between two friends. Suspension bridges have a much longer **span** than most other bridges.

Some bridges are only for people on foot: footbridges cross over streams; skyways are closed bridges that con-nect buildings.

A tower holding the cables of a suspension bridge

Unusual Bridges

Some bridges are a bit unusual. The Pulteney Bridge in Bath, England, was built more than 200 years ago. It has stores on top of its arches. Ponte Vecchio in Florence, Italy, is even older. It was built in 1345 and has survived many wars and floods. The gold jewelry stores on its bridge deck are world famous. ❖ From the 1700s through the 1800s, rain and snow rotted many wooden bridges. Some builders tried to protect their bridges by putting walls and

By the time workers finish painting the Golden Gate Bridge, it is time to go back to the beginning and start again.

roofs on them. Some of these covered bridges still exist in the

northern United States and Canada. ❖ Some bridges move.

Early drawbridges were used to cross castle **moats**. If a castle

The famous Golden Gate Bridge in California

was attacked, the bridge was lifted to keep the enemy from crossing. Later, drawbridges were built so tall ships could sail under low bridges. When a tall ship approached, traffic on the bridge was stopped. The two arms of the deck moved up and swung open. The boat passed through the open arms. These kinds of bridges are still used.

Some bridge arches are nearly 1,700 feet (518 m) long. That's almost as long as six football fields!

Tower Bridge is a famous drawbridge on the Thames River in London, England.

A boat passing under the deck of Tower Bridge

17

Building Connections

A lot of work goes into building a bridge. Engineers must decide what type of bridge to build, where it will go, and how long it will be. They might choose to build with wood, stone, iron, steel, or concrete. ❖ Building a bridge can take many years. It took

John Roebling was the chief engineer on New York's famous Brooklyn Bridge. Sadly, he died before the bridge was completed.

four and a half years to complete the Golden Gate Bridge between San Francisco and Oakland, California. Bridge building can also be dangerous. Bridge workers today often

wear safety belts and harnesses to keep from falling long

distances if there is an accident. About 20 workmen died

building New York's Brooklyn Bridge, which opened in 1883.

Manhattan Bridge and Brooklyn Bridge in New York

❖ Today, bridges link people and cultures around the world. They connect cities, states, and countries. They cross streams, rivers, and lakes. One bridge in Japan even crosses a sea! Engineers placed bridge towers on small islands to support the bridge. In the future, who knows where we might build bridges? One day, maybe

The longest suspension bridge in the world is the Akashi-Kaiko Bridge in Kobe-Naruto, Japan. It is 12,828 feet (3,910 m) long.

we will be able to drive all the way across an ocean!

Trains cross a river on this suspension bridge

Building a Better Bridge

This experiment will compare the strength of a beam bridge versus an arch bridge.

What You Need

Two thick hardcover books of the same height
A piece of typing paper
20 pennies

What You Do

1. Stand the books upright, about six inches (15 cm) apart, and lay the paper across the top.
2. Pile pennies, one by one, in the middle of the "beam bridge" until it falls.
3. Now, curve the paper upward to form an arch and stand it between the book supports.
4. Pile pennies on the "arch bridge" until it falls.

What You See

The arch bridge holds more pennies than the beam bridge. The force of the pennies pushes down on the center of the flat paper and makes it fall. However, the curved arch moves the downward force of the pennies away from the center to the sides. Pushing against the supports makes the arch stronger.

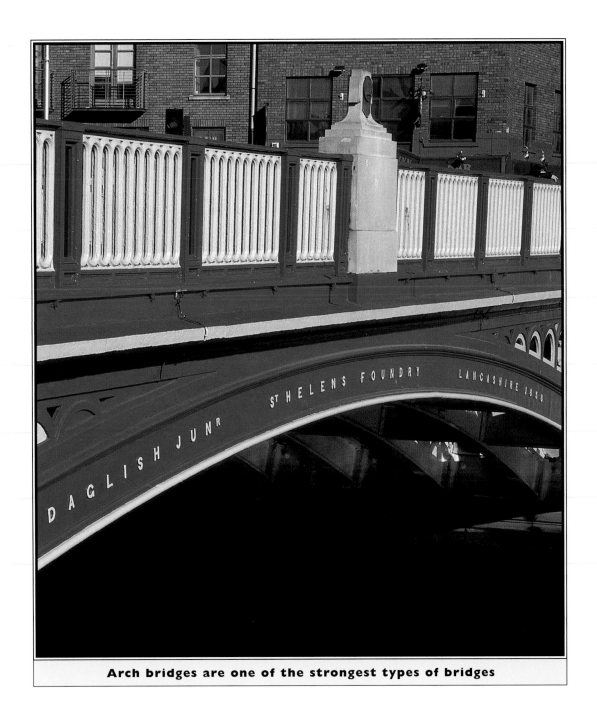

Arch bridges are one of the strongest types of bridges

INFORMATION

Index

Words to Know

arch (ARCH)—a curved structure

diverted (dy-VER-ted)—turned aside or sent in a different direction

engineer (en-juh-NEER)—a person who designs and builds machines or structures

moats (MOHTS)—deep, water-filled ditches that surrounded many old castles

span (SPAN)—the length between two objects

Read More

Baxter, Nicola. *Bridges*. London: Franklin Watts, 2001.

Hill, Lee Sullivan. *Bridges Connect*. Minneapolis, Minn.: Carolrhoda Books, 1996.

Oxlade, Chris. *Bridges*. Chicago: Heinemann Library, 2000.

Sturges, Philemon. *Bridges Are to Cross*. New York: Putnam Publishing, 1998.

Internet Sites

Building Big
http://www.pbs.org/wgbh/
buildingbig

Super Bridge
http://www.pbs.org/wgbh/nova/
bridge

New York State Covered Bridges
http://members.aol.com/covbr